THE VIEW
FROM SATURN

ALSO BY ALICE FRIMAN

Vinculum, 2011

The Book of the Rotten Daughter, 2006

Zoo, 1999

Inverted Fire, 1997

Driving for Jimmy Wonderland (chapbook), 1992

Insomniac Heart (chapbook), 1990

Reporting from Corinth, 1984

Song to My Sister (chapbook), 1979

A Question of Innocence (chapbook), 1978

THE VIEW FROM SATURN

POEMS

ALICE FRIMAN

Louisiana State University Press
Baton Rouge

Published by Louisiana State University Press
Copyright © 2014 by Alice Friman
All rights reserved
Manufactured in the United States of America
LSU Press Paperback Original
First printing

DESIGNER: Michelle A. Neustrom
TYPEFACE: Tribute

LIBRARY OF CONGRESS CATALOGING-IN-PUBLICATION DATA

Friman, Alice.
[Poems. Selections]
The view from Saturn : poems / Alice Friman.
   pages ; cm
ISBN 978-0-8071-5722-0 (pbk. : alk. paper) — ISBN 978-0-8071-5723-7 (pdf)
— ISBN 978-0-8071-5724-4 (epub) — ISBN 978-0-8071-5725-1 (mobi)
I. Title.
PS3556.R5685A6 2014
811'.54—dc23

2014002304

The paper in this book meets the guidelines for permanence and durability
of the Committee on Production Guidelines for Book Longevity of
the Council on Library Resources. ∞

✳

To Great-Aunt Sadie, wherever she may be, who told fortunes
with cards and never gave up hope

Until at length old Saturn lifted up
His faded eyes, and saw his kingdom gone,
And all the gloom and sorrow of the place . . .
—KEATS

What then must we do?
—TOLSTOY

CONTENTS

Tracing Back 1

I

The Brain 5
How It Is 6
The Night I Saw Saturn 8
Bluer than Blue 10
Now 12
Vexed 13
Troubled Interiors 14
Rock-a-Bye 15
Ironing the Brain 17
Ars Poetica on Lava 19
The Acolyte 20
Visiting Flannery 21

II

The Skin 25
Kindling 26
70 over Nothing 28
The Argiope 29
Visiting the Ruins 31
Transfixed 33
Round and Around 34
Because You Were Mine 37

Adrienne Rich 38
At the Rothko Chapel 39
The Runner 41
Tybee Island 42

III

The Joker 47

IV

The Hands 55
The Pitiless Drift 56
Aunt Nellie's Walk 57
Time Was . . . 58
Coming to Terms 59
Payback 61
Falling in Line 63
Silhouette 65
Tarnished 66
Coming Home 67
My Father's Chrysler 69
Three Takes on a Couplet by Neruda 71

V

The Tongue 77
The River 79
Coming Down 81
Letter to New Zealand 82
The Fireman and His Wife 83
Watermelon 85
Medea, Intent 86

The Real Thing 89
Behind the Door 91
Cleo to Antony 93
The Birthmark 95
Red Camellia 96

POSTLUDE

Of Crockery and Mythic Tales 99

Notes 101
Acknowledgments 103

THE VIEW FROM SATURN

Tracing Back

In the history of reading,
there's many a cracked heart,
lost letter, stopped clock, cut wrist.
Any cursory push through poems
or stories and you could trip
over the drownings
or the heap of crushed
petticoats fluttering on the tracks.

To the bookish, I say *careful*.
What's between two covers
can creep beneath covers.
Any thief worth his prize
knows how seduction works:
ingratiation: the innocent pull
of words, that belly crawl
of language. What do you
think that first slither was
coiling the winesap,
so lovely, our girl was forced
to write it down, there
on the underside of leaves.
Hers, to sneak past the terrible
gates, hidden in the rustle
of her figgy apron: the key
to what she didn't know yet
but would be looking for
in all her troubled incarnations.

I

The Brain

The brain always knows
where you are. A triumvirate
of eyes, ear canals, tiny nerves
in the joints phones in regularly.
I'm biting my cuticles. Over
and out. Practicing the tuba. Or
guess what I'm doing in bed with
all this flesh? The brain knows.
That's why you can pass
the neurologist's test: clap hands
in the dark. They'll find each other.

Using twenty percent of the body's
blood supply, a billion gray cells
should be good for something—
discovering a cure, unearthing
the great gray owl of wisdom, re-
reading Aristotle's *Ethics,* remembering
where I left my keys—something
other than smug in their aerie
this Tuesday afternoon being clever
when I'm standing at the window
watching the hawk's persistent
shadow, circling.

How It Is

Late October
and the pitiless drift
begins in earnest. And all
that whispered in the pockets
of summer's green uniform
is shaken out and dumped.

My mimosa knew, for wasn't
that death fingering the leaves
all summer? Yet the tree
plumped its pods, spending
all July squeezing them out,
going about its business, as did
the slash pine and loblolly,
spraying pollen—coating
windows, cars, filling every
idle slit with sperm.

What does life mean
but itself? Ask the sea.
You'll get a wet slap back-
handed across your mouth.
Ask the tiger. I dare you.

And *your* life, with its
tedium of suffering, what
does it mean but what it is?
And mine—balancing
checkbooks and *whomping up
a mess of vittles* as my son
used to say. My son, the funny one,
the always-hungry-for-supper-
and-the-happy-ending-
I-was-never-able-to-give-him one.

Who am I to write the user's manual
for a life, except to say,
Look at trees, dug in and defiant.
Be like the river. Stick out your tongue.

Why not? What's to lose
when what's to lose is everything?

The Night I Saw Saturn

Crossing the Pacific, flying backward
into perpetual night, and all night
one light on in the plane, a young man
beneath, scribbling. I am looking out
the window, the glass prism that shatters
the stars, and we at thirty thousand feet
not flying up but seemingly across
and headed straight toward it—Orpheus
of the night sky—the rock that sings.

What is he writing, that man
who can't sleep so doesn't even try,
stuck in an inner section, unable
to indulge in a window reverie, leaning
his head as I do against the glass?

The night I saw Saturn was because
I pleaded. *Before I die I want to see . . .*
and the astronomer complied, there
on the top of Mauna Kea, and me
shivering in all the clothes I had
and hanging on because I couldn't
see my feet, so dark it was as I set
my eye to the metal eyepiece.
Then, true to the pictures in my
schoolbooks or the planetarium's
mockup, only luminous, radiating
more energy into space than received
from the sun. Ah Saturn, grandfather
of Love, what do scientists know
of the light that lights the pearl? Beauty's
absolute, cold white and burning in the sky.

And now, this man, the only light
in the plane, ringed by huddles of sleepers
as if he were guardian of the oblivious
awake for us all. How furiously
he bends to his work. How lovely
the light lingering on the shock of his hair
holds him—incandescent—reflecting in rings.

Bluer than Blue

Scientists say cosmic dust
is the cause, or vapor, wave-
lengths or Lord Rayleigh's
law of scattering. But I say
the reason the sky turns
bluer in September, pouring
down a rush over every roof
and tree, is Earth herself—
our own girl—gussied up
in her best blue atmosphere
for her autumnal tango
with a star.   Lie still, spine
flat to the ground, turn
off the radio in your head,
hold your breath and hush.
You can almost feel her,
tipping back in a rolling
ecstasy of air, chiffon sheer
as Salome's blue tease, so deep
you're sure you could fall up
and into it the way you would
a couch of three wishes—
every want you ever wanted
found in those loosening
wrappings of her pleasure.
Oh, that such bluer than blue
were enough to forget the leaves'
droop and softening, now
that we are in the vortex,
the winding down of the clock.

Better to imitate the twirling
earth, flaring out her silks
while the spider spins her last,
each day squeezing shorter
from both ends. What else is to do
but dance, the way leaves will
come November, the way
my sweet young thing—the only one
who ever loved me—whirls me
each night in his arms?

Now

Once upon a time
there was no such thing as time.
No before, after, or last week.
No cause, effect, push, pull,
elbow room or jostle. And I was there
and you were there and every atom
of rock and leaf and dog was there
jammed together tighter than lockup
or a screwed-down jar. All was
nothing but a big now that swelled
to aching, not able to hold anymore.
And when it finally burst
like an orange full of juice
wet with a bang not a whimper,
time began. Past and future took off
in a line, galaxies raced out
and away. And light began its travels.

For us in our little corner,
now broke into thens and whens,
what-ifs and all the in-betweens.

We needed bridges and hyphens
to fill the gaps, electricity to arc the void,
parentheses to hold it in, leaving us
lost, having to maneuver here to there
and back again. And hours came to hang for us
heavy as snow-sagging wires. Heavy
as eyelids and the sleeplessness
of trouble. For what is blood
running in circles compared to time
that knows only zoom and straight ahead?

Vexed

I like the word *vex*.
Not honey in the mouth
like *barrette* and *gorgeousness*
but raw edged. I like *tonic* too
and *flunk,* words easy to say
but hard to swallow. *Burdock,
punk, mock, fang.* Brave
words that begin by playing
about the lips and end
low in the throat, packing
a blade. A watch out!

I like words that can live
on their own. Unadorned.
Detached. Their own sentences.
Ah, but you will read this
as Rorschach, the poet
vexed and embracing it.
Better *vexed* than a sibilance
like *silence* which begins
at the front, makes a tiny trip
down, then seized by what it sees
backs up like a flunky, slithering
through gritted teeth, and out
the way it came.

Troubled Interiors

When fish wake in the sea
fin-shaken by whim
or tide, what a confusion—
subject as they are to the wee
switch in the brain that makes
permanently opened eyes see
or not. But how enviable the dreams.
Lidless projections on big wet screens,
unlike our own troubled interiors.

My mother too, in the high hours
of her dying, could not close her eyes.
The once-bright hazel, transfixed
under a yellowish glaze. The lower lids
drooping inside out like buntings
of raw meat. Animal under the ice,
frozen in sight of the hole. I could not look.

Fish stare, stare of the all-knowing,
stare of retribution—or was that imagined—
as I laid a cool wet cloth over her eyes.
For her comfort, I said. Then holding her hand
and singing the songs she'd always sung to me,
I sang her, blindfolded, out of this world.

A good daughter? Let me tell you.
The eye of ice flings enough light to read by.
Even now, six years later, lying here in the dark,
I can still make out the words. *Liar. Fraud.*

Rock-a-Bye

Not even a smother-mother
holds on to her children
tighter than do these trees,
buttoning each to each twiggy
finger so they'll feel safe
flipping and flying about—
acrobats in a delirium of green.

I stand at my window
watching the May winds
have their way with these
rooted mothers giving in
to being bullied and tossed,
pantomiming the great
drama of grief and keening
to indulge their progeny, tender
with infancy, their first ride.

We live in a sea of air—
breath moving on the waters
animating all things. See how
the wind lifts the limbs
to reenact the ocean's heave
and swell. How new leaves
flutter about the crowns
like giggles of foam, and all
is up and down, gallop and glide,
carousel horsie and *whee*.

Then my daughter calls.
My own long-stemmed Lilly—
grown from the heart's bulb
and nurtured behind the briars

of vigilance—to say she's found
a lump. What an ugly word
to take over this poem. To squat
on its one-syllable immensity
and not move.

Ironing the Brain

Sometimes I'm tempted
to set my brain on the board,
trembling like a Jell-O
slipped from its mold, plug in
my old GE and flatten her good.
One thump and a glide. Never mind
the sizzle. Scientists say, smooth
all fissures and bumps and you
are looking at sixteen square feet.
Enough to carpet a telephone booth.

Imagine, sixteen square feet of
brain underfoot to tap and shuffle on
while waiting for that "Hold on,
I'll call you right back" call
that never comes. And you know
at that moment—a sudden
jab in your arch, your brain trying
to tell you something—you're going
to live the rest of your life like that.
Suspended, waiting. And for what?

Now that I'm getting on, I propose
a better use for that postage stamp
of a rug: a Martha Stewart bath mat
in pewter or pearl: a confection
of synapses and tufts, dendrites
and meningeal branches woven
into a fluff. The concentrated
power of the human frontal cortex
flat on its back in fringed surrender.
What a blessing. Perfect syntax
and the luxury of the right word right

there all the time. And me, standing on it,
dripping, the poem rising like a watered ivy,
pure and unbidden between my toes.

Ars Poetica on Lava

> So much depends...
> —WILLIAM CARLOS WILLIAMS

The night I picked my way
across the lava slicked by rain
in the moonless dark, all past
and future sliced away
like bread. Nothing existed
but the blade of my held breath
and the flashlight probing
the black and roiling rock
for a safe place to place
a sneaker down. One shoe
after the other, disembodied
from the feet they were tied to,
with orders to swing out, land,
grip, and pass me on.

Two hours it took to cross
that stretch of Stygian black,
having no thought but the need
to prevail, upright. Now I know
what it means to balance
a writer's life. Each footfall,
each stopping point, a fulcrum
around which the body teeters
and sways: a high-wire act
demanding concentration—
the chattering mind delivered up
blank as cardboard with a pinhole,
dependent, in the pit-dark, upon one
thin thread of dazzle coming through.

The Acolyte

> And the fire that breaks from thee then . . .
> —GERARD MANLEY HOPKINS

Spring, and the birds are flocking,
revved up and zooming
around the house in a sleeve
of air, bouncing off windows
then pouring into the holly tree
to gorge on red berries. Wee
gray engines with brown tufts,
too wet out of the shell for
thoughts of wooing. Only eating
and being part of the vow that is
each other. Born to it, this watery
flow of multiple births moving as one—
this communal orgy of worship.

The holly is Argus-eyed,
each berry, each holy tidbit
winking red, signaling
from dark leaves: Eat me, stuff me in,
shit me out. Spread the good news.

But what of the celebrant
too heavy with bliss, too loaded
with gobble and gulp, who hit
the window? The *ah! bright wings*
that never rose? The baby dinosaur
blessed with appetite, slammed
by a boomerang of light?
I tell you, *My heart in hiding*
Stirred for a bird. The split breast.
The stained feathers. Gash. Gush
of red spill. Splotch of sour and unripe.

Visiting Flannery
ANDALUSIA

Across the pond and up the hill
from where I sit, the lady's house—
her room of crutches and ugly drapes,
the flat and sorry pillow. Her Royal
turned for concentration to a wall.

I come often, greet the orphaned space,
wave when I leave. But today, Good Friday,
I wonder what she'd think—this Yankee
heretic, two generations from steerage,
scribbling by her pond across from
the screened-in porch where afternoons
she'd rest, enjoying her peahens'
strut and feed. How old is too young
with so much left to do? Even the barn,
reliving her story of what happened there,
is buckled to its knees.

Suddenly, a flash from the water—
fish or frog—and I too late
to catch the shine. The Georgia sun
dizzies my head and I am no saint.
Nor was she, although there's some
who'd unsalt the stew to make her one.
Still, I like to imagine—before the final
transfusions and the ACTH that
ballooned her face past recognition—
the two of us sitting here, watching the trees
sway upside down in sky-water, ecstatic
in the bright kingdom she refracted in a drop.

Funny how two pairs of eyes fifty years apart
make one in sight: a country pond

floats a heaven, and patches of trillium
spread their whites, laying a cloth for Easter.
She smirks. Easy imagery. We do not speak,
both knowing what won't sustain when clouds
roar in like trouble, the trillium inching
toward water, fluttering like the unbaptized
lost, or the ghost pages of an unwritten book.

II

The Skin

Beneath the white,
polar bears have black skin
to absorb what heat there is
in a world of chill.
                    Never
mind the designer cashmere
catching the eye. It's skin
that counts. The necklace
riding the breath registers
nothing of the oily touch
fumbling with the clasp.
Only the delicate nape
grasps the whole under-
story, there where the fine
gold hairs read Braille and
memorize.
                Peel a sunburn.
Under is the blush of all
your old embarrassments.
Even soles, shy in shoes,
are tickled silly with
what's afoot. We take in
through our skin. What wife
doesn't know that?
                    Each night
when he comes home, I lean
in to him, unbuttoning his coat
to reach the warm. I hush him
with my mouth. I am reading
the news. Lip to lip, skin to skin,
what slights he has endured—
what little murders.

Kindling

There's part of the breath
that never changes, no matter
what you eat. Dependable
as fingerprint, that label
that says this is you, none
other. Open your mouth
and an airy boat of DNA
launches into the conglomerate.
Toot toot, make room.
Here I am.

                But the berth
the boat has rocked in
too is what we are: sixty
percent water, upright puddles.
Why, if not for hearts and
all working accoutrements—
vessels and valves—we'd be
walking Niagaras pooling
at the bottom. Sloshed
to the shins.

                As for earth,
some things are better left
unsaid—dandruff, hangnails,
nose hair, the reason for
outhouses—not to mention
tissue composition, hydro-
carbons, and salts. *Ashes*
to ashes, dust to dust: what
remains, stripped of the fictions
that kept us warm.

                        Of fire?
Ah, there's the rub. Not
the two-sticks variety

but the zizzing business
in the attic. Neuron-speak:
synapse to spark, sputter
to flare until the brain
storms under the skull. Flame.
Conflagration. What the other
three are broken and consumed for.

70 over Nothing

Today, a leaf on the path, big
as a dinner plate but curled up
and juiceless as if its DNA
forgot how only two days ago
that crunch under my foot
was being ordered to *Hang on.*
It stopped me in my tracks, so lost
in thought I was, wondering
how anyone could still live
with such a number—cuff
squeezing to the bone looking
for a sign, a twinge, an anything
to fill the space below the line
where that bottom number
is supposed to be, and unable
to find one, delivering a shrug,
an *I give up.* So too that leaf
feeling the stubborn mother-hold
suddenly loosen and let go.
Yet she kept breathing, faint
yes, then desperate, as if breath
were treasure to be ripped out
of air and grappled for. Crying?
Sure, lots of it. Daughter, son,
brother. I can swallow that.
But seventy over nothing? All
vessels gone slack? The aorta,
flabby as an old woman's upper arm?
But she was young. She was young.
What does that have to do with it?

The Argiope

Between the weeping cherry
and the porch, the argiope
floats head down at the center
of an enviable patience.

Her egg sac—little ochre
marble, little kindergarten sun—

pasted to the rail: another
Pandora's hope at the bottom of the box
one more artist won't live to see.

The cherry cannot hold her
even with all that weeping
any more than it can hold its pinks,
or October its fool's gold.

One September night
she will dismantle all her silks
and disappear.

✷

In here, on the desk
by the window,
an old photograph—

cousins, five of us, frozen
in the slanted sun
of our last free summer.

How patient we are
squinting into the camera

and grinning because we were good
and were told

except for the one
in her new kindergarten dress
with the white collar, the one
caught in a worried look

as if she were already
staring out this window,
watching the unthinkable going on.

Visiting the Ruins

Imagine the missing sounds.
A salt lick without the scuffles.
Stolid maples without their
raspy spray of leaves, dense
to the height of them. A child's
scramble.
              Then picture papyrus
or clay tablets or even this paper
blank, leaving not even a doodle
to be dug up, or a line, nor ring
of fieldstone to mark the quirks
and manner of the one who held
that instrument, quill or stylus.
Or pen. The fields plucked clean,
the parade grounds emptied,
all connections cut.
                Why else
does one write, but to deliver up
the vacuum and fill it. Not
to fix or finish, for what was
is sealed off and done, but to
wheel it out again on its own
cobblestone streets. And given
one's own slippery notions
of truth, to erect a stop sign
that says *here:*
              Here is the table
where the child drank her milk
and figured her decimals. Here
the arch under which soldiers
came, their boots ringing the stones.
And here in the weeds behind
the mechanic's shop, a child's

nightgown, tossed aside like
an afterthought of no account, as if
deeds were porous, and the gag
and thrashing legs were only smoke.

Transfixed

What does day want
but blue—all cloud complications
pushed through sweet
as blues through a trombone
or water riding the elbow
under a sink.

What does night want
but simple—A into slot B,
C into D and all constellations
clicked into place, not a ruckus between them.
Each star a saint, subsisting
on its diet of burning.

But in between,
in the gentle hour before dawn
when time spins pointlessly
on its spindle and sky doesn't
know coming or going, what could
that want? Outside my window
winter twigs arch before a backdrop
of roseate light. A scroll
unrolled. A silk to read
and read by. Peach blossoms
of winter, having slipped
their petaled outlines
and escaped.

Round and Around

In the old days before
earbuds dumped music
directly into your ear canal,
there was radio. Love songs
bleating from every station—
torch songs, misery songs,
eat-your-heart-out salt songs
rubbed in your every wound.

A girl thing. Fourteen,
and here come the lyric lessons
of you're not good enough.
A lesson as necessary
as your first mascara and
the skin you love to touch.

Boys played ball in the streets.
Girls clung to their radios
and pined. Whom shall we
renounce ourselves for, yearn for,
be shamed by, deserted by,
forgive? That is to say—
whom are we doomed to love?

*

So I'm dancing. An Irish boy
and he's singing "That's My Desire"
into my hair and holding me too close
for being fourteen and not knowing
what exactly a *rendezvous* is
except to say I want one and everything

else that song's dishing out in the sweet
body of the boy singing it.

*

And *the music goes 'round and around*
Whoa-ho-ho-ho-ho-ho
And it comes out here:

Charlie Greenberg, the redhead
who got caught in ladies' underwear.
His father's business. And the guy
whose name I can't remember—
worked his father's grocery, said
he saw my face among the tins.
Me and Campbell's soup. Peas.
Heinz ketchup. One hot tomato.

So there I am, swaying in Mama's
living room to the latest promise
on the radio. Nineteen and ripe.
Miss Juicy of New York City
dancing my discontent, the way
I will all my life. Even now—

Listen to the jazz come out

one hundred and six years old
and still playing Ginger Rogers,
the trees outside wind-dancing
with me. Forget their yearly
baby crop of leaves. Deep-rooted,

trees are stuck in the old days—
shimmying fringes, dipping
and flipping back their heads
like Janis Joplin on a tear
or the single-leg inflatables
in front of the used-car lot on Jefferson,
screwed in place but hot-damning it
all day and into the night, being equipped
with hot-air blowers at their feet—
roaring, just like me.

Because You Were Mine

One day in the home, my father
was struck by a bolt of philosophy—
split down the middle to reveal the last
two bits of his reason. Ninety years
in shadow and all at once at the bottom
of the canyon, the Colorado glints in the sun.

Poor Daddy, turning on his last spit,
wearing diapers and gumming peas.

He wheeled his chair in close, knee
to my knee touching, took the hand
last held when I was five.
All barbed wire down between us.
The bloodshot eyes, for once,
not racing, not looking for a doorway out,
but locked to mine as if he saw, at last,
the constant known as *daughter*
he'd been looking for.

Now, twenty years later,
I am no closer to understanding
the words he spoke, heavy with import
as a museum plaque: *You know, I loved you,
and I hated you. Because you were mine.*

But I know truth when I hear it,
just as I know I am his masterwork.
No wink of water lily or sunflower in a jar,
but tangled snarls, scribbles and broken lines.
What else could he have done, given the demands
of a blank canvas: that blizzard in the head
he was lost in?

Adrienne Rich
1929–2012

She came to read her poems—
those straight-talk towers
of brick and mortar—and to speak
of the cracked earth and seething
rock beneath them. Each poem,
a requiem for the rubble she stood in:
the twentieth century that cast her
and cost her. A serious woman
who spent her life spending every
thing she had.
                Outside the room,
winter maples organized themselves
against the sky, and sparrows
pecked at what they could find
as they had always done. And we,
of the chicken salad and buttered roll,
folded our linen napkins, laid
down our silver, and hushed—
waiting for gold.
                But as soon as
she mounted the stage and leaned
to the microphone, we leaned back
and away in our chairs. You could
barely discern it, but yes, back away
is what we did, for in her voice
and in the match strike of her eyes,
she flared fire, and I saw again
the ghost of the old refinery, the one
off Township Line Road, its towers
lighting the night sky, each burning off
in one pure flame the impurities we were.
You see, she spoke true. She spoke witness.
And we knew it.

At the Rothko Chapel
HOUSTON, TEXAS

What is the portrait of Nothing
but the night sky without a star.
An abstraction real as a hit on the head
or a hunk of bread bitten off hungry
with the back teeth.

But if Nothing means absence,
that's another story. Then the portrait
must hint at what beat there, the last thrum
before dying, the last shadow of the last
rope frayed out.

Fourteen black paintings
in a surround with no escape. Fourteen
portraits of the face of Nothing or
of an absence so unbearable, Nothing
saw fit to pour in.

One can't help but want a spit
of yellow or a Pollack drip of red
to latch onto, to say, this being a chapel,
something must eulogize the life's colors
of what mattered.

Outside the entrance, a display
of holy books—your choice to borrow,
take in with you. An amulet to ward off
the emptiness by holding a book
which denies it.

Rothko knew what he was doing.
Sit here and look. Here where the benches
are hard, the floor stone, blocks of stone

trailing footsteps of fading echo
unlike the colors

you strain to see but can't,
being bled out—that Wednesday, right
across both arms. What he said art is:
The simple expression of a complex thought.
Simple. Straight as a razor.

The Runner

Having nothing to think about
but the fact of nothing to think about,
nights like these she lies in bed
staring into the dark. Her mind
running in circles around
that emptiness. Her only alternative—
to chew her rag, that grimy
reconstruction of slights
and wasted days.

Outside the window
the moon mocks.

She gets up, paces, stops
at the loaded bookcase—
old remedy—studies
the configurations of dust,
constellations of dried auguries.
Old tea leaves in a cup.

How deep is this rut she's run?
Deep as gravity. The blank space
she races around congealed into a solid
the way a black hole becomes
the mother you can never get out of.

Tybee Island

In January, she drove
to the end point of the earth, rented
a room with no television, no phone.
She wanted only to walk by the sea,
to find in that old shine and display
the familiar key back on its hook.

She hadn't counted on a storm
wanting her naked, tugging at her clothes.
She hadn't counted on the tides, fresh
from tsunami, still in an iron frenzy
sicced on by the winds. She pushed on.
Gulls lined up, intent as paparazzi
waiting for news, then rose in one
great hoop and cry reporting to the sea.
What was to fear, having sifted through
the lost beaches of childhood so long,
each shell, each *bawk bawk* matching
a twin in the red pail of her memory?

The sky sneered in contempt,
rammed a fist of wind into her back.

Never mind beaches of the past—swells
off Montauk, the racing waters south of Piraeus
where foam is ermine and all the world of wet
royal and electric. Here was stagger, wind-
bloat and fury driving the sands before it
like ghosts of beasts fleeing on their bellies,
a howling anger pushing them down.

Gray bone in a gray soup.
Who could find her? No light

shafted these clouds, no Bernini burst
of promise and dove. The horizon's fog
cementing up its one red eye.

A woman stands facing the sea, holding on
to all she has, and the sea, struggling
to heave itself up, teeters on its watery legs,
and with a roar and a suck
tries to take it all back. Gulls
blink their yellow eyes. They know
what they know: here, where each cry
slaps a wet mockery back in her face,
where the winds' mounting displeasure
sledgehammers down to crack open the sea,
here is the interior of a stone: a boulder
split inside out and alive: her old dead mother
thrashing in anger, spitting in her chains.

III

The Joker

A house of cards has
no window. No kitchen,
no tarts. The queen, with all
her hearts, holds no more sway
than a four. The king, equal
to a deuce or that knave,
the town crier with a bell,
announcing a royal beheading.
This is the house of the joker,
trickster of the dark carnival,
scepter of misrule, dedicated
to the chop. This is the house
of whimsy—a balancing act—
built to fall.
              I shuffle the cards.
Time for my nightly game
of solitaire, that pasteboard
horse I've ridden for fifty years,
the deck sticky with constancy.
A dog barks, a clock ticks.
Black five on a red six, red
seven on the black eight.
Wait. The aces are loading
but the one-eyed jack who
waxes his golden hair will
not turn up. The queen of clubs
drops a flower on my grave.
She is my mother. The king
holds a sword to his side,
threatens to use it. Relegated
to the box, the joker, reader
of fortunes, smirks.
                 Great-
Aunt Sadie too told fortunes,

visited once a year at night
to hawk her policies. Peed
with the bathroom door open,
bloomers hanging a bunting
between her knees. Grandpa's
sister, Grandpa's shame—
bucktoothed Sadie, old
as the old country, skin like
boiled chicken, gray hair
wild around her head as if
she stuck her toe in an electric
socket. Mama rolls her eyes—
bedtime. Oh, the danger. Not
to be there when Aunt Sadie
reaches into her black purse,
that mystery squatting at her feet
like a patient filing cabinet,
big and bottomless as the trap-
door to forever. See how
she hauls it into her lap, un-
zips, rummages, then
pulls out that little red box,
slips off its rubber band to
snap around her wrist, winks,
and shakes out the cards.

                        Look
at any deck of cards. See
how the joker prances about
masquerading as a jester
to jolly the royals—silver
bells on his cap, pointy shoes.
The joker's grandfather, no un-
forgiving Puritan like mine,

but Tarot's Fool, so busy
poetizing flowers he'd follow
his own babble off a cliff.
Measure the fall: Fool
to faker to jester, jester to
joker—free to say anything
and excused in advance. Lord
of anarchy, writer-in-residence,
boss of *all fall down*.
                History
engraves in spirals, the needle
buzzing like a doorbell—
a summons one needn't answer.
The joker will take care of it
from the peephole of his privacy.
Here's a story:
                On the Pyrenean
marble top of the pedestal table,
Madame Irène lines up the cards.
It is Paris before the war,
Madame's grand salon—
the white hexagonal room
where six Aubusson tapestries
illustrating La Fontaine's fables
fill the six panels of the walls.
Ladies put down their cups,
press to her side, or kneel
on the water-silk *voyeuses*
to watch. Navigating the room,
the light from thirty scented
candles settles on our heroine,
and all chat stops. What can
the cards tell of the future

of this house and the Madame
whose worth will founder
in scandal? The Master
has retired to his collection
of porcelains, the only love
he has left to love. The joker
will not show his face tonight.
He doesn't have to. His best work
is done in the dark.

                        Aunt Sadie
lays out the cards on Mama's
kitchen table—the usual ten-
card spread. Her six-dollar
watch flashes in the light
of the overhead bulb. Her eyes
flick over the cards. She is
reading her fortune. Aunt Sadie
doesn't know from marble tops
and gilt-legged chairs, nor has
she ever heard of La Fontaine,
but she knows fable. She knows
slow and steady wins the race
and when to gather up the cards,
shuffle, and lay them out again,
for like the princess and the pea,
she's made uncomfortable
by tests of purity. The queen
of spades—even at six I know
the old-maid card when I see it—
she tucks back into the deck.
She is looking for someone else.
And when he shows up as he
inevitably does, she kisses the air,

gathers up the cards, buttons
her make-do sweater, clicks shut
her purse, and is gone.
                          The joker
appreciates odd visitations:
the race-car driver invited
to dinner, the one Madame
will run off with—the children
abandoned or taken from her,
grandchildren she'll never see
who'll die in the camps. The joker
is intrigued with consequences—
what happens when someone
just drops in. Lately he has taken
to dropping in on me. Could be
I remind him of someone—
skin loosening on the bone,
hair gone wild. He's begun
whispering to me at night:
past accomplishments, his best
of the best. I tell him he's just
gathering material for a sort of
New & Selected and I want
no part of it.
                    After Sadie died,
a cedar chest was discovered
in her rented room. A hope chest
filled with hand-embroidered
pillow slips, sachets, nightgowns,
lacy lady things still waiting
as they had for seventy years,
ever since she'd been sent out—
too ugly for marriage even to

the Sauerkraut & Pickles man
on the corner of Orchard
and Delancey. Yes, sent out
to scrounge up a living selling
insurance, climbing tenement
stairs, knocking on doors for
her fifty cents. But always
she believed he would come,
dazzling in his full regalia—
the Jack of all hearts, the Jack
who would turn around at last
to take her as she was, holding
out the leaf he held in his hand
as if he had just picked it up
that day in Central Park, the first
leaf of autumn when the world
pours down, sad and most beautiful.

IV

The Hands

    After conception everyone spends
    one half hour as a single cell.

Imagine—
smaller than a decimal point and already
ready for long division. Each hand
wanting its own arithmetic to get as far
from the other as possible. The left's
penchant for roses, the right's for
the fork.
          Yet how often they search
each other out to wring in despondency,
clap in awe, make mirror images
to cradle a beloved face. How like brothers
smacking each other around, or sisters
picking at each defect.
              Only at night
are they still, the body balling up to be
one again, each part coming home limp
to center. See how the old in their chairs
stare into their laps, each gnarled, papery hand
holding tight to the other the way they did
that first day in kindergarten, knowing something
big was about to happen.

The Pitiless Drift

Here in Georgia, summer
arrives in April, hunkers down
and doesn't move. By late September,
leaves, weary of gasping for air
and fighting the forest's impatience
for straight up and naked,
give up their chatter, and hang
limp as ducks in a Dutch painting.

So when the tenth month comes,
henna bright and tooting her honey horn,
they're not fooled. They know clarity of purpose.
For didn't they too have it once—riding the new air,
tossing their reflections to the forest brook
in their May day, heyday of pure light
and shimmering?

And didn't they gulp it down, opening
their mouths to eat the sun, and wasn't
that priestlike job their joy?

Oh, how will death find us
if we are not what we were?

Footfalls of slanted light
linger in the wards of the dying—
solace of the purple aster, tangle
of thistle and red berry. See,
in the mirror of the winding brook,
the queen of siege and necessity. See
how she pauses, head cocked and listening.
The faint echo of her machine gun
stuttering through the forest, as all around her
in a feathered blessing, the gold ducks fall.

Aunt Nellie's Walk

An oscillating fan. That's
how my Nellie walked.
A metronome on tiny feet—
hips sashaying side to side,
swinging in importance.

Now she sleeps in a chair,
unable to recall how she once
marched behind the fire truck
in the parade and danced
the two-step with flowers
in her hair. Her mind, a blowout
in a bowl. But given a nurse
with biceps and a bully streak
to hoist her up, glue her
to a walker, and command, *Walk*—
you'd see it. Even if her feet
couldn't move and she were reduced
to reflex under the cotton gown
tied in back, there—beneath the flesh
trembling to be off the bone at last—
that built-in hint of impudent wag.
Oh Lord, give us back this day
a little butter for our bread.
What shame to have such flaunt
gone from this world. The tap
tap of summer sandals,
the swinging counterpoint
of her arms, the lilting seesaw
of her hips. I swear, that woman's
to-and-fro could hypnotize a watch.
My Aunt Nellie, soul of propriety,
queen of good causes, trailing
in her wake such endearing treason.

Time Was . . .

The first thing I did
was take down the clock
running dutifully on its one cell
of battery and move the hands
forward, so the day could tick itself
out correctly. And as if no crime
had been committed in the interim,
no honest grocer shot, no house
foreclosed, no mother locked frantic
in the search for a missing child,
time resumed its pure pace,
chipping off the required squares
of space as before—numbers
straining toward twelve, one hand
chasing the other under the shadow
of the thin red whip driving the whole
terrible mechanism.
                        And suddenly,
like an apparition called back
from a great distance, there we were—
the blue-white sea air, the first starts of stars,
your watch ticking to itself on the dresser.
And how we said we were beyond
time, as if one could declare a truce
with what's next. There shall be
no what's next, we swore, only honey,
and what's next falling into it slow and caught
as in amber. How could I have imagined
then, such silence. Such drowning.

Coming to Terms

In the short interval
between cannonball and boulder,
bonk, blackout, and drown,
there's little time for thought
or remembrance—
rod and reel and the timeless
drifting of days. All gone
in a hurtle. The fallen one—
cowlick sweet, a pebble—
hardly big enough to vex
the meandering stream.

Or the fleeing thousands
sucked out to sea: flailing
matchsticks unable to appreciate
the science talking heads chew
up for us to swallow down
so human time can be flipped
back, bright side up again.

Why not? The river
returns to reverie. The sea
to its grudging obedience.

Look, says the butcher, life
is blood and bone running
mindless—a headless chicken.
Not so, says the baker. Life
is sugar or plain, jelly roll
or stale bread. No indeed,
says the candlestick maker
buffing his silver, life means art.
But the drowned say, life

is the thing we clutched—
our own murderous baby—
it being all we had
when the sea rose to claim us
and the boulder hardened
against us and would not yield.

Payback

Coming up for air, the river
boulders are showing their backs.
Old fat guys not seen in years,
a razorback of weeds, lewd
and itchy dry, springing from
their cracks.
                Ripples of nervous
water—what little remains—
fawn like flunkies in sequins
while the blue heron that used to
fish these shallows, lifting his feet
precisely and placing them exquisitely
down, has disappeared, wanting
no part of the show.
                  Global warming's
six-year drought has flipped
the bottom to the top, and the old
bosses from witness protection—
humpers of mud, cons of coverup—
are through with hiding. Walking
these banks, I follow the point
of nature's finger. The more lovely
the scene, the more in-your-face
the undersides. A river shrinks
and in so doing glitters like a last-
ditch effort. And the gray behemoths
that wallowed at the bottom, cousins
to the three-ton hippos of the Zambezi
spraying their shit with their wedge-
shaped tails, firing it off in aromatic
bullets of revenge, squat now
in all their former glory, flashing
their glacial history.
                If science

will not suffice with all its statistics
and charts, let us try to remember
how to read in the old way. Look.
Far as the eye can see down the river's
length—the cold, first stones of prophecy.

Falling in Line

Consider wallpaper.
Barely perceptible, but see—
threading the roses, the line
where they were joined
to make a garden.

We live in a world
of lines—by-lines, lifelines,
off-lines, on-lines.
Dotted lines, deadlines,
your lying line of love.

Klee said, *A drawing
is simply a line going for a walk.*

So is a poem. Ditto
a life. Danger happens
when you find yourself
not out of
  line, or in
    line, or even
behind lines, but

between lines—edges
so close you can't get out.

The lines under your feet,
there, where planks
tongue and groove,
creating crevices
where dust

gathers to itself,
beyond reach of vacuum
or broom, pulling you in
until you too
are too safe and gradually
colorless. So deep
even the light licking the floor
can't find you.

Silhouette

Undressed, her body
wanted dancing. Behind drapes,
draped only in air without belt or bind,
her grace—the sweep of a bird—
outbloomed even the garden
she outlasted. Undressed,
she joined the assemblage
of stars
for like the night
she had thrown everything off
to burn on the axis
of her own turning. She danced
undressed
and without shame, for she was old
and the tune in her head
was subtraction.

Tarnished

What she hated most
was the trembling, the hands
gone all papery, the intestine's cringe,
and sleep glaring from the corner
where it would not lie down.

She knew the trick: chew it up
and swallow. Not to play old-lady
blissful, wheeled smiling in her chair.
No need for that. Only, like the brass
lamp on her dresser, to give back a little,
a bit of shine. But truth was, by then
she had no shine left. What else
could I have done, the only one
left who loved her? I rubbed her raw.

So she turned away. *The Soul
selects her own Society—Then—
shuts the Door.* What she wanted
was perfection, the interior she worked on
all her life: frost crawling the windows,
shutting her in. The hours, thick
as silence, thin as the press of her lips.
Dust motes stirring the gloom.
My presence worth no more than that.

They said she was lost.
She wasn't lost. *I* was lost—a cutout,
a black silhouette abandoned at the far
edges of her ice. See that black hole?
That's me, the genie, still hovering with
polish and rag, waiting to be called back.

Coming Home

Early March, and a pale
sky tightens down spiteful.
What clump of green there is
seems vulgar, out of place,
superfluous as last year's
newspaper or the curtain
in that front window, shredded
into abstraction. And if he felt
the target of a pair of eyes
or a ghost giggle from behind
a hedge, after sixty years away,
the mind plays tricks. He blinked,
wiped his glasses, blew into
his hands against the cold,
then lingered on the porch,
listening for the whine
of the battered Electrolux
being jerked around on
its leash, the dusty swish
of a rag. Nothing had changed—
the old push-pull of stasis,
the ugly guy wires of stock still.
But he'll not enter, not trust
the old key to the old lock.
He knows better. For what if,
for story's sake, he's tempted
to brave the long hallway again,
past the yawning closet of
mildew and wet mackinaws
and smell? Then the dash to
his room and down on his knees
to peer under his bed the way
he used to, looking for creatures

that fidget in the dark, waiting
just waiting to snatch him up?
How pitiable those monsters
of childhood turned out to be.
As if anything could have spirited
him away, rescued him from this.

My Father's Chrysler

My father was a philosopher.
Filosof, Mother called him,
his long underwear drooping
at the seat. But still, between
black moods or the strap
he threatened us with and his
Saturday morning dancing
the dishes in the cupboards
and singing in a voice to rattle
the neighbors while reaching
under Mama's girdle for a pinch,
he was a student of great minds:

Imagine a building on fire. Three
vehicles arrive at the same time—
fire engine, ambulance, mail truck—
who'd have right of way? Answer?
A mail truck, of course, being federal.
I imagined flaming bodies leaping
off ledges clutching invitations
to birthday parties not to mention
bills, Macy's catalog. But surely
he was right. He was my father.

I remember watching him watch
a storm come in, glued love-
struck to the window as if seeing
for the first time himself in the mirror
of that furious sky. What was he—
this man I matched my steps to,
calling myself the son he never had—
but a two-bit Byron without a battle:
a romantic stuck behind the wheel

of a panel truck marked *Clover Towel*,
making deliveries, a Chesterfield
dangling from his lips. But always
a feel for the beautiful. A Platonist
hankering for the ideal—the crowning
storm, the invisible absolute, the never
to be attained: the Car.

Dear Reader, we are not talking
about any car—a Chevy, Ford,
Dodge, a Japanese anything. We are
talking deeper than metaphor, purer
than Ivory Soap, and more powerful
than his brother's Oldsmobile, his brother
the bully who could bash him back
to childhood where it all began and would
if he got the chance. A white car.
A dazzling car. A knock-your-eye-out
absolute of a car: proof and judgment
that years of slogging and glad-handing
for customers, long johns for winter
and sweating summers would add up
to something that even if he didn't know
what, at least it would be shining.

He never got that car nor the motorized
wheelchair he would have had to settle for.
He ended up stuck, diapered in a chair.
A philosopher with a cane that he wielded
like Excalibur, the unsullied sword, waving it
in your face and trembling with rage.

Three Takes on a Couplet by Neruda

1
Let us forget with generosity
those who cannot love us,

who would put a grade
on all our sitting downs

and standing ups. Who seek
like a can opener to pry,

to peer inside and catch us
in all our inconsistencies.

What else can one do
in such a case but turn away?

Only the rain is allowed entry.
Only the rain and the lover.

2
Look at this morning's sky
blotchy with cloud, the sun

trying so hard, falling in splinters
all over the lawn. Lighthouse

that cannot hold its beam together.
If we, the poet says, must forget

those who cannot love us,
how *can* we, given this

splintery light roiling over us
like tide in an under water drown,

when to forget—generous
or no—means setting the clock ahead

into our own oblivion
which will come soon enough.

3
First reading, you would think
he meant forgive rather than forget.

But no, his comfort was to forget
and concentrate on what exists

and will go on without us—

the sea, the pines, the *tang
of sun and salt,* where from

*the mortuary of the seaweed
rises the smell of birth and decay.*

Tell me, Signor Ghost,
what beach did *you* walk

where the waves came in
and backed out without you?

Raised their humps to fall
at your feet before sliding away

leaving a shell, a bit of weedy
remembrance in the sand?

What is the world without us in it?

Where did other people take you
that you forgot that?

V

The Tongue

> Taste buds are replenished every two weeks, each one
> knowing how to inform the brain what the mouth takes in
> and what enzymes are needed.

Every morning after I brush,
I stick out my tongue to admire
my buds. Those wise, discerning
little clones plugged into the brain
by who-knows-what voodoo rite
of chemistry. Baby gourmets
born already appreciating
the delight of fried sweet potatoes
with a perfect cheeseburger.

Having only two weeks to live,
there's scarce room for insult.

Impatient in the clutch of a wet
happiness, wee nestlings open wide
for the savor and smack of good
food—the last thing you want
before you can't want anymore.
Grandma, ninety-nine and blind,
still relished a bit of onion on her plate
when all she could manage for dinner
was a dollop of mashed salmon
and three green beans.

Let those of us in poetry's holy
orders speak not in tongues but of
tongues—that nursery of bumps,
nodes, nubbins, pimplets of pleasure:
buds so small one needs a microscope,

but cheek to cheek, petal to petal,
weave a flowering—a red carpet
for good bread, oranges, morning
coffee, French toast with almonds,
my sweet love's watering mouth.

The River

I stood in my grandmother's kitchen
watching my mother roll her mother's hair.

She wanted a permanent.
The hair a white mist, nothing more.

The rollers, pink. Her scalp
pink too, but different. I was

twelve. I thought no one could be
so old and trembly. And pink.

I thought a lot when I was twelve—
I thought nobody thought the way

I thought, to be so old and still want.
What could be left for her to want?

Her face a crosshatch of lines.
The head, the hands. The terrible shaking.

Little ghost, if you could speak, you
whose eyes look at me now—tell me

my charge. You are sixty-two years gone,
surely nothing but splinters left.

What do you order me to write
other than what I know? That nothing

is as cruel or sweeter than the shortness
of our days. That flesh clings,

refusing to be destroyed even as it is.
That, yes, there were three of us,

and after, to celebrate your curls,
we had tea in the yellow cups,

and the best Russian coffee cake
in the world—your favorite—

with eddies of walnuts and cinnamon
roiling through, dark. Like a river.

Coming Down

At high altitudes the heart rises
to throat level, clanging for service.
The body—#1 customer—needs oxygen,
the red blood cells scurrying like beaten
serfs not delivering fast enough: supply
and demand, that old saw.
                            Remember
struggling to make love under six blankets,
my heart banging so hard it threatened
to knock me out of bed, and you
in socks, ski hat, and four sweaters, fighting
for breath? When relating our story, paring
it down for parties,
                    let's leave those parts
out. Say we went to South America
for pre-Columbian art and Machu Picchu.
Mention the giant condors, yes, but not how
they floated up from Colca Canyon
like human souls circling in great flakes
of praise
            nor how I cried, reaching to bridge
the unbridgeable gap. Say that one shivering
night we visited a thermal pool, but not
how slippery as twins tumbling in the womb,
we sloshed together under Andean stars.
Or how nose-bleeding or heart-pounding
and laboring for breath,
                        always always
we reached for each other. Practice the lesson
of the body in distress: the heart knows
how much leeway it has before demanding
its due. Waiting in line for the Xerox calls for
giveaways of more supple truths: cartilage, Love,
not bone.

Letter to New Zealand

Yes, of course I remember
the clouds that hid the tops
of Auckland the day before
I left, as well as your fingers,
heavy as quartz on the nape
of my neck then sliding fast
as raindrops on a window
down my back only to stop
as if they too, lost in fog,
had to pause for the heart's
instructions. And how after,
I stood at the hotel window
that became my gazing place,
remembering your telling me
of Kupe, the original voyager—
how after he died, his wife
was asked to speak the story
of the first sighting. *A cloud,*
she said, *a long white cloud.*
And I knew what I heard
was true, true and sad
at the same time.
                         So yes,
I think of you, but more
of the cloud she saw hanging
suspended over the length
of your whole country like
a canopy or flying carpet
stalled and out of gas, and how
it took a woman—the first
woman—upon seeing it
to understand immediately
the relationship between
cloud, shadow, and regret.

The Fireman and His Wife

FOR VIVIAN AND HENRY

Sensing the exact amount
of pressure her bones could bear,
he'd fold her to him to still
her fluttering—the crumpled
wing she had become. They say
he left her once, found her too
spunky (his word), and all this
love stuff was nothing but guilt.
But maybe not. V-J Day
he came home whistling, never
to leave despite her flood of
rotten luck: bad heart, Hodgkins,
the shakes, and the straw that sucked
her dry—losing the kids.
                         Egg,
chicken, which comes first—
the job or the proclivity?
All I know is, he figured out
how to gentle her to him
not from practice or habit
but because how could she live
without him? She was his four-
alarm, his midnight panic
creeping up the stairs. If you
asked her what motivated him,
she'd wink in her cocky way,
and in a whisper—for at
the end, whisper was all
the arsenal she had—declare
only that he was *kind*. But
what kind of word is *kind*
for a hook & ladder man
who battles terror face to face?

Ah, but there's terror and then
there's terror. Who's to measure?
Later and alone, he paced
the cell of his backyard each
night. And maybe for the first
time focused not on the pin-
points of fire as he was trained
but the sky's unstoppable
flood of emptiness gushing
out between that made him, not
two weeks after she was gone,
suddenly clutch at the weight
slamming into his chest as
if embracing it, like that
Greek who clung to his boulder,
who stuck to the struggle of
his stone because, like moss,
he couldn't live without it.

Watermelon
FOR ALEKOS

Small as a bocci ball, dark
green and striped, the latest
in Kroger's arsenal of seven-
a-day and rich in lycopene,
but thirty years ago you were it—
karpúzi—and I'm tap tapping
my head, pantomiming your
new name, *Karpúzi*, for stupid,
for melonhead, for how could you
when by witness of moon-melt
and star, we crossed hearts in
sign language/love language,
the inky sea pounding out my
deposition: *I'll return in a year,
steal the money if I have to.*
What kind of sieve lets go of that?
Not the blushing bougainvillea
eavesdropping by the bus station
when I left, or the shrieks
of pipers and black-backed gulls
egging on the tides, or the wet
silver slapping of a morning
catch, and the cracked split-
nailed hands struggling the hook
out of the mouth, Greek
filling the air like falling flakes
of Scrabble, happiness tiles
to make the words that would
have kept you waiting. Even now,
given a morning's clean and
breaking hour, it all comes back
as I did. And you, gone on
with your life, opening your big
dumb arms, wading right into it.

Medea, Intent

1. Jason

Ogle, grin, kiss me blue
then finish up. Tomorrow
the door closes and locks. Never
mind the shadow beneath my pillow,
never mind the taste of salt
you complain of left in the mouth.
Without you I am sponged clean.
The basin water splashes clear.
Despite what you murmur,
you've not doomed the tight poppy
that is my life. Orange is the true color
of the storm. A wind is coming
high-pitched and terrible. Be afraid.

2. The Children

Little snail, and you, mama's plump bone
asleep in the terrible shadows.
Poppies of my love. To cut, to taste
the salty spurt, oh, what blizzard burns
in the doomed glass? You stir.
Hush, don't be afraid. I am clear
as the water splashed on the washing stone.
Kiss me. Kiss me in your sleep.
(Lock shut my heart.) Listen,
my wine glass is on the table.
When you wake, stir the rim to singing.
I've left a song for you about heroes.
Dragon's teeth and orange fire.

3. *Hecate*

Come. The poppy burns
in the glass. I am not afraid.
Do not murmur like the broom
on the stones or threaten high-pitched
from the shadows of my sleep. The snail
winds in the terrible lock. My wine
tastes of salt. The hero storms in, splashes
in the basin water next to my bed,
sits on the edge, grins, spurts his filthiness.
Come, finish me. I have had enough.
My pillow smells of oranges.
The mop in the corner, tight and clean
as a burnt bone. I am ready.

4. *Æetes*

Father, what was I
but the moody poppy of your house,
a mop or bony broom singing
in the corner? I sent you back
your true treasure, cut up, piece by
splashing piece to burn in the pyre for
the murmuring crowd. Kiss him for me.
The filth, the terrible treasure, I keep
beneath the washing stone where the snail's
slime has turned the gold to orange.
Now there is too much to clean.
My heart plumps with shadows.
I'll not speak with you again.

5. *Jason*

The storm has come. The finish
terrible as your truth. I have cleaned up
my table, my wine glass, the splashed
stones. I have twisted the mop.
There is no grin in me. I am done.

I have taken my cut treasures
wrapped tight in their pillowcases.
See how I'm kissed by their blood.
I leave you *your* treasures: The burnt bone
of your new life and the locked-up secret
you tricked me for. I left my shadow
murmuring in the orange tree. My wash water
in the basin for you to drink.

The Real Thing

You can always tell the Greek
from the Roman copy, the same
way the lover knows the lover
in a crowded room and how
not to get in the way
or fill the space between
with finger food or chat. To just
let it come—head on and straight—
the real thing.
                I was nineteen,
New York, and he wasn't even
Greek but second-generation
Polish with a wife on vacation.
(How tacky can you get?)
But if he wasn't the real thing,
he was as close as I ever got—
love's seal and stamp, my first
journal entry, my preview
of coming attractions, my
press your head to the X
on the wall—desire.
I still see him walking away
down Eighth Street in the day's
last lingering light. Golden he was.
Even the sun was stuck on him.

All these years, persistent
as a jailhouse dream, he's been
with me—my favorite CD played
on long car trips, or in the tube
of an MRI when the only itch
you're allowed to scratch
is a bite of memory. And when

I finally decided to push delete,
for after all, enough is enough,
I couldn't. So burned in he was—
his left wrist bone, his arm's sun-
kissed treasury of fine gold hairs.

Behind the Door
FOR R.

Letter left in a pocket, strange
earring in a glove compartment—
such simple things—and the world
implodes. Wife rattling around
a house that used to be home,
child staring at her plate, picking
through her peas. The lover lost
without love's current that had
like a river carried him so long:
the sweet rush he'd lived in—
tent in the woods, motels in
how many towns. And, of course,
the unnamed, the dear someone
somewhere sitting by a phone,
daring it to ring. Do not think
I am a stranger to this story:
the promises, the required apologies,
the ritual baring of the jugular.

Oh friend, be warned. The heart
may not stay in storage long,
riding an iron track, obedient
as a shooting-gallery duck.
A heart wants to be used, fed,
nourished on nuzzle and whim,
practicing the skills it's learned
of whisper and cunning. It needs
to believe that on any ordinary night
before the pitiful throbbing stops
and the body—that new amazing toy—
is laid out and displayed like a plastic
floral arrangement, a rocket

will slip in low under the radar,
roaring and flashing lights: the stars'
own emissary. And why, but to test
the line of *Do Not Cross*, the line
of unprofitable, for the heart is not
mollified by notions of safety nor apt
to thrive on a diet of crackers and milk.
It wants what it wants: what's behind
the door, knowing full well the key
swings on a rope hanging from one's
own neck. That's the place, isn't it?
Such sweet skin, there in the neck's
hollow where she'd lay her mouth,
cupping the pulse as if to drink
and hold inside her all that ecstasy,
that mad hammering before it dies away.

Cleo to Antony

Can we settle this dispute
quiet-like, reach in tandem
for a conclusion? No?
Then let me be queenly about this.
No more nosing at throats
for a scuffle, no more wound-
sprinkling salt, no more sabers
rattling in the clothespress.

Let's take a poll. Who wants
more blame? More heart's
spillage? I miss your hammer toes,
you miss my pinkies, I miss
your big sword, you miss
my bathtub, big as a mixing bowl
for two. Cannot we imitate
the rabbit in the race and stop
for a nap? Lose, and in so doing
win back what we had? Already
our troops have deserted, and
what allies we've salvaged
from the wreckage have sold
their allegiances. Octavius
and his legions roar at the gates.
Sic transit gloria mundi. It's true,
the world has shrunk to this—
a dung beetle, a pebble, a herpe
that will not heal, that even the fates
have surrendered a bottom lip to,
has entered the world's stage
to direct our end. The challenge?
To be bigger than he is, bigger

than the history he strides on.
Oh my wild one, what do we have
left but each other? Let us pluck
a pearl from the crown of despair
to light our way in the dark—
a miner's lamp glowing
down the tunnels of the ages,
saying here—where our flickering
story haunts the walls—here
is Love. Temple and triumph.

The Birthmark

He sleeps, rowing his boat of breath
down the night's long stream of hours.
With each intake, a click of oar in the locks,
then the long *psssss* across trembling water.
I press to his side, adjust my breath to his,
hoping for contagion. The opiate blessing.

Outside, emptied now of the leaves
that breathed for them—those nervous
complications—trees lift their ribs,
hoisting their hollows for the moon
to fill with silver. See how they imitate
my love's labors—or is he, stripped
of the day's busyness, mirroring theirs
while that naked rock in borrowed clothes,
that looking glass of reflection,
pours down, dignifying everything?

I turn back the covers, unbutton
his sleeping shirt, the zebra one
bought our last day in Africa.
Africa, mother of beginnings where
the moon herself was born, ripped
from the Rift Valley, the cesarean scar.

Come, I say to the moon, meet the new
Endymion, shepherd of term papers
and syllabi snoring in the Latmian cave
of our bed while I count the sheep.
Forgive us. We serve a shabbier world.
Shine on him nonetheless, lay your silver
hand on his chest, on the two-inch circle
of no pigment over his heart—that gene spot
of mute I have tried to kiss into words
a hundred times. That human cry of hollow.

Red Camellia

The bush has reaped her reward:
she cannot hold up her arms. A salute
to her location at the corner of the house
where the sun is beguiled to stop all day,
and the wasp tending its cells under
the shed roof swoons at the riot of red
multiplying in its compound eyes.

March has finally given way,
and spring in Georgia, primed
with lascivious plumpings,
has sent word: we've little time.
The camellia has waited all year
locked in her thin verticals
for the sun's first hot speech.
Now she answers—one voice
blowing from two hundred mouths.

Love, I want to talk camellia talk,
quick, before summer's endless
conscription in a green uniform—
that stifling march into fall.
Speak to me. Be my sun, my day star.
Look into my eyes until I'm lost to sight,
then juice me up red and barbarous:
a phalanx of redcoats, a four-alarm fire.
I'm tired of pork roasts and ease
in an easy chair. Bring me one more
season. A reason. Bring it in your hands.

POSTLUDE

Of Crockery and Mythic Tales

What's seen from the corner of the eye
teases our notions of reality
the way the sliver from what's left
of last night's dream
proves fondle enough
to shatter a plate the next morning
while washing the dishes.

If real contains other than
what's to stub your toe—trees
outside the window, the broken
shards at your feet—
then add the wounds of childhood
never to be scabbed over
and safely stowed under a scar.

And don't forget the jolt
that lives in shadows playing off
a wall or the sudden flash of light
bounced off a polished table.
What difference if what flickers
from the periphery is actual
or the mind's projection? Maybe

that buzz in the brain is creation's
running narrative, the holy book
of empty space. Nights
when the ceiling locks down
and the palm at the end of your wrist
repeats and repeats its lines, it's the mind
that spins out deliverance.

A bedtime story. A horse with wings.

NOTES

Epigraphs: The quotations are from Keats, *Hyperion,* book I, ll. 89–91, and from Tolstoy's book *What Then Must We Do?*

The information about the body in "The Brain," "The Hands," "The Tongue," and "Ironing the Brain" was obtained at the Body World Exhibit, which I was privileged to visit when it was at the Franklin Institute in Philadelphia.

"The Acolyte." The quotations are from Gerard Manley Hopkins's poem "The Windhover."

"Visiting Flannery." I am referring to Flannery O'Connor and her farm, Andalusia, where she spent the last years of her life.

"Three Takes on a Couplet by Neruda." The couplet I am referring to is in his poem "Sonata with some pine trees," which can be found in his book *Extravagaria.*

"The Joker." All information about Irène Cahen d'Anvers (1872–1963)—her house, her marriage, and her unfortunate history—comes from a visit to the Musée De Camondo in Paris.

"Tarnished." The quotation from Emily Dickinson comes from poem #303, "The Soul selects her own Society—."

"Round and Around." "The skin you love to touch" was ad copy for Jergens Lotion. The song lyrics that run through the poem are from "The Music Goes Round and Round"—one of the many popular songs from the twenties and thirties that my mother used to sing to me.

ACKNOWLEDGMENTS

I wish to thank the editors of the following journals, in which these poems first appeared:

American Literary Review: "Now"

Boulevard: "Round and Around" and "The Tongue"

California Quarterly: "The Acolyte"

Cortland Review: "The Real Thing" and "The River"

Field: "The Skin" (as "Dermatology")

Georgia Review: "*Ars Poetica* on Lava," "The Birthmark," "How It Is," "Letter to New Zealand," "Red Camellia," "Rock-a-Bye," "The Brain," "Behind the Door," "Aunt Nellie's Walk," and "Coming to Terms"

Gettysburg Review: "The Pitiless Drift," "Cleo to Antony," "The Runner," "The Hands," "Tracing Back," "Bluer than Blue," "Payback," and "Time Was . . ."

Margie: "The Fireman and His Wife"

New Letters: "Ironing the Brain," "Visiting the Ruins," "Vexed," and "Watermelon"

Shenandoah: "Coming Down," "The Joker," "Visiting Flannery," "The Argiope," and "Coming Home"

Southern Poetry Review: "Three Takes on a Couplet by Neruda"

Southern Review: "Falling in Line," "The Night I Saw Saturn," "Transfixed," and "Adrienne Rich"

Subtropics: "Medea, Intent," "Tarnished," and "Tybee Island"

Valparaiso Poetry Review: "Of Crockery and Mythic Tales"

"Because You Were Mine" is reprinted from *Prairie Schooner* 82.3 (Fall 2008) by permission of the University of Nebraska Press. Copyright 2008 by the University of Nebraska Press.

"Kindling" and "Troubled Interiors" are reprinted from *Prairie Schooner* 84.2 (Summer 2010) by permission of the University of Nebraska Press. Copyright 2010 by the University of Nebraska Press.

"At the Rothko Chapel" is reprinted from *Prairie Schooner* 85.3 (Fall 2011) by permission of the University of Nebraska Press. Copyright 2011 by the University of Nebraska Press.

"Tracing Back" won a 2012 Pushcart Prize.

"The Night I Saw Saturn" won the 2011 Gretchen Warren Award from the New England Poetry Club.

"The Fireman and His Wife" and "Watermelon" were included on the *Verse Daily* website. "Time Was . . ." and "Behind the Door" appeared on *Poetry Daily*.

Some of these poems were anthologized in the following publications:

Alhambra Poetry Calendar 2010, ed. Shafiq Naz; *The Southern Poetry Anthology, Volume V: Georgia*, ed. William Wright and Paul Ruffin (Texas Review Press, 2012); *Visiting Dr. Williams: Poems Inspired by the Life and Work of William Carlos Williams*, ed. Sheila Coghill and Thom Tammaro (University of Iowa Press, 2011); *Women Write Resistance: Poets Resist Gender Violence*, ed. Laura Madeline Wiseman (Blue Light Press, 2013).

∗ ∗ ∗

I am grateful to the *Georgia Review*/Bowers House Literary Center, the MacDowell Colony, and the Carson McCullers Center for Writers and Musicians, where many of these poems were written, and to all the friends and fine writers who have stood by me through the years—Dale Kushner, Jo McDougall, Roger Pfingston, Marilyn Kallet, Laura Newbern, Martin Lammon, Patricia Waters, Marianne Boruch et al. I am especially indebted to Andrea Hollander and David Huddle for their invaluable help in ordering this manuscript. To my husband, Bruce, my "sweet young thing," a kiss for his enduring patience and devotion.

www.ingramcontent.com/pod-product-compliance
Lightning Source LLC
Chambersburg PA
CBHW030142170426
43199CB00008B/173